MW01289745

Rewire Your Mind

Stop Overthinking. Reduce Anxiety and Worrying. Control Your Thoughts To Make Better Decisions.

Steven Schuser
steveschusterbooks@gmail.com

The fact that an individual, organization of website is referred to in this work as a citation and/or potential source of further information does not mean that the author endorses the information the individual, organization to website may provide or recommendations they/it may make. Further, readers should be aware that Internet websites listed in this work might have changed or disappeared between when this work was written and when it is read.

For general information on the products and services or to obtain technical support, please contact the author.

Table of Contents

Introduction

The Advantages of Knowing

To rewire your mind, the first step is to understand how your mind works. In order to simplify something, you have to know what to simplify.

Have you ever made up your mind about changing your thoughts? Did you get washed away by a *hell yeah* feeling as Metallica played a badass rock song in your head while you mapped out your big plan? For example, maybe you decided to exclude negative thinking from your thoughts, be mindful, and try your best to stay balanced and not lose your temper. You followed your plan well enough for one or two days—you were cool, and when you felt the explosion coming, you took a deep breath and swallowed it back. But on the third day, something bad happened, something more annoying, sad, or frustrating than on the first two days, and boom:

negativity, anger and impatience invaded your mind again. Your head got filled with thoughts like "stuff always happen to me" and "I'll never be able to be a positive thinker," and so on.

As you can see, by the time one negative thought ends, another one has captured your worried mind: the realization that you were complaining again despite your life-changing plans of eliminating dark, sorrowful thoughts. Suddenly, the Metallica jam of the previous day transforms into a sad aria, and you fall deeper into the pits of disappointment at not being able to keep up with your resolution.

Stories like this happen very often with us. We set our mind to accomplish something, but the same mind sabotages us. We vow to be nicer to our over-controlling mother, or our sloppy spouse, or our chatty-but-kind-hearted colleague, but all our good intentions get flushed down the toilet when we lose presence in the moment and forget about the vow. Then we react with usual negative, snappy, or mean attitude we so want to avoid. Only when the red clouds disappear do we realize that we experienced another neural hijacking. As a consequence, we start having a fight with ourselves inside our mind. Our mind struggles, blames, craves improvement, and becomes angry for not improving.

Can this neural chaos be tamed somehow?

This is debatable. The best chance one has to dissolve the chaos in their brain is to get to know how it works.

Knowledge—and thus understanding, acceptance, and compassion—dissolves the Gordian knot. You have to know which thoughts you should stop fighting against. Some thoughts are evolutionarily coded into your brain, and you need to stop trying to change them. They can't be eradicated, but they can be tamed and minimized. How? This book will help you answer this question.

When I was five years old, I thought that taking a breath was some kind of personal deficiency, some vicious form of OCD (obsessive-compulsive disorder) that I should eradicate, otherwise people would think I was a weirdo. As a result, I focused on not taking a breath. Somehow, the impenitent craving to repeat the weirdness with my nose came back after a few seconds. I focused better the next time, but after a minute or so, it came back again. I went to my parents, crying and saying that I was crazy because this stupid snuffle wouldn't stop. I told them that I tried to stop it, but it kept coming back. You can imagine their bewilderment while listening to me. They told me that the stupid snuffle keeps me alive, and I should never try to stop doing it again. This is how, at the age of five, I learned that breathing is normal.

Ten years later, I learned that the most primitive part of the human brain that we share with all other species—the root brain—is responsible for regulating breathing and other basic life functions. This ancient brain doesn't think or learn; it's the autopilot that keeps our body running, granting us survival.[i] My childish attempt to stop the stupid sniffing, therefore, was in vain. Later in this book, we'll see that stopping breathing is just as impossible as some other fights we have in our head regarding our thoughts.

- Which thoughts can be changed, and which are those we should change?
- How should we pick our fights with our mind?

- Is the fight worthwhile, or does it just create greater chaos?
- Isn't simple understanding more helpful and enlightening?

Sometimes simply knowing that what we think about is not wrong or abnormal can grant us peace of mind. This leads to acceptance, and the mental knot will dissolve by itself.

Over the years, I learned that having negative thoughts is neither abnormal nor unnecessary. What's more, sometimes they are completely grounded, and if I'd lived a hundred thousand years ago, they'd be indispensable.

This is why I chose to go through the rudimentary activity of our minds in the following chapters. Yes, minds—both the thinking and observing mind.

The Advantages of Not Knowing

I get many emails from readers asking how they can shut down their negative mental small-talk. You know, that kind of annoying cerebral chitchat that tells them they will never find a good partner, or their business will never hit the six-figure-per-month income they desire. Before you start thinking something's wrong with you, let me tell you that we all have this kind of self-talk. Even those who score a happiness touchdown most days face diminished self-esteem struggles once in a while.

Reading Mark Manson's controversial bestseller, *The Subtle Art of Not Giving a F*ck,* confirmed something for me that I'd suspected for a long time, but had never really thought about in depth.

People sometimes don't know what they are talking—and therefore, thinking—about.

What do I mean here? Exactly what I wrote. We sometimes have no idea why we act the way we do or say things in a certain way. Sometimes we are totally calm, but in the next moment, we lose our cool and become anxious, depressed, or contrarily, very happy. We talk about our happiness or anxiety, but we don't know why we feel it all of a sudden (there is an explanation, and I will write about it in the next chapter).

Sometimes, out of nowhere, anxiety crawls into my thoughts about my fragile and awfully young writing career. What if I'm not good enough? What if people don't like what I write? What if the Earth will be invaded by alien cyborgs, the Internet collapses, and I sit in total existential isolation, not being able to feed my wife and children (most of my income is thanks to the online world today)? Or what if my wife divorces me and leaves to live as a hippie with her yoga instructor, Josh? What if my children become serial killers? Holy cow, alien cyborgs, serial killers… Josh? Where did *these* thoughts come from? I don't know, and maybe that's for the best.

I'm clueless about why I'm thinking about these worse-than-worst-case scenarios. Who knows what the future holds? Maybe soon I won't even be excited about writing anymore and I'll start doing something different. Maybe in 20 years, having serial killers kids will be great because they will be the ones who defeat the alien cyborgs. My wife and Josh? I still can't figure out a positive side to that—but I'll try. The future is so unpredictable, and we change so much as people. It is impossible to predict if the worst outcome of a present fear is a good or bad thing in the future.

Similarly, we can't be totally sure if today's happiness won't become tomorrow's sorrow.

Occasionally reminding myself about my own cluelessness helps me overcome existential dilemmas about my future. Whatever my mind says about tragedies in the present is probably wrong.

There is a twist in this story that I hinted in the previous lines. If our mind is unreliable and we don't know what we're thinking, and our thoughts might be wrong, that applies to all thoughts: *negative and positive*. People question their negative beliefs much more frequently than they do their positive ones. However, questioning both is equally important. Questioning positive beliefs brings you back to Earth, keeps you from becoming overconfident or arrogant, and most importantly, eases your mind.

The higher the stakes you set for yourself, the greater pressure you'll feel to live up to them. Mark Manson addressed this issue with the following example in his blog post. "If I believe I'm destined to be the next Leo Tolstoy or Albert Einstein, that is a LOT of [...] pressure to live up to.

And that pressure is likely to cripple me and turn me into a neurotic [...]. That pressure is likely to close me off to any and all important feedback. I wouldn't be able to write a word. I'd second guess every single sentence, including this one."

Positive events don't really teach us lessons. They may make us feel better about ourselves. Briefly, we will feel that our hard work to get what we just achieved wasn't in vain. But positive events do something else in our brain: they set our expectations and standards higher. Today's maximum will be tomorrow's minimum. For example, if you make $500 more this month than usual, you'll feel happy for this month. But next month, when thing go back to normal and you make your normal salary again, you'll feel you lost something. You made $500 less than last month, after all, even though that was not your normal salary. It is easy to make good things the new standard.

There is a fable I really love. It goes as follows:

Once upon a time, there was a man and his horse. The man only had one horse, and the horse ran away. Immediately, his friends began to express their sympathy to him in his time of misfortune, but the man simply responded with a "let's wait and see" attitude as to what might be in store for him in the future.

After a few days, the man's horse returned and had 20 wild horses following him. Again, his friends reacted quickly, ready to celebrate his good fortune, but the man kept his same "let's wait and see" perspective.

It wasn't long before the man's luck changed for the worse when one of the wild horses kicked his only son and broke both of his legs. The man's friends rushed to console him, but he continued to want to "wait and see" what would happen next.

The country went to war, causing all of the young men to be drafted and ultimately killed, but because of his broken legs, the man's son wasn't drafted, and so his life was spared. The man's friends expressed their joy and gratitude that his son was safe and alive. The man still held on to his "wait and see" outlook on life.[ii]

We rarely think as this man does. Whether events are negative or positive, we can never be sure how will they evolve in the future.

The advantage of accepting that you don't know as many things as you think you know can relieve you from a lot of mental clutter. If your goal is to have a rewired mind, the best you can do is accept that you're sometimes wrong, and that's perfectly fine. The time you invest in self-flagellating thoughts can be spent much more productively, like in taking action instead of thinking about the unknowable future.

Why do I say we don't know what we think?

A few centuries ago, astrologists believed the Earth was in the center of the Universe and everything else revolved around it. My people believed that the short, black-haired man who liked to scream German words had good values upon which they could build a superior nation.

When I was a child, I believed my parents when they told me carrots would help me whistle better, and with my improved whistles, I would attract pigeons. I also believed spinach made you stronger, but I resisted eating it to avoid getting disproportionately large forearms like Popeye does. As a fourteen-year-old, I thought it was lame to be nice to girls and that disinterest was the way to win respect.

While I was dating my first girlfriend, I believed we'd always be together. When she cheated on me, I thought I'd never forgive her. When we broke up, I was certain I'd never love anybody as much again. And for some weird reason, I was convinced that no one would love me as she did. My second girlfriend loved me much more than I loved her. I thought I was responsible for her feelings. I felt I was a horrible person for not loving her more. From carrots to love, I was wrong.

I don't believe there are absolute rights or wrongs; there are only things you experience to be right or wrong for you based on your values, and your freedom to practice your rightness can expand to the point where you violate someone else's freedom in doing so. Excluding extreme negative values, we can agree that "right" or "wrong" are subjective. Based on different past experiences and values, people will have different answers to the same questions, and none of these answers will be better or worse than the other.

Even our own answers might be different today than what we would have said 10 years ago. When I was a teenager, I was convinced I should be mean to gain respect. Today, I believe I was wrong back then. People have a history of being wrong about things they once believed to be right. You have a history of being wrong about things you once believed to be right too.

You have a superpower. This superpower is the ability to think. Your brain works all the time. It has to think about something 24/7. When it becomes puzzled as to what you should think about a situation you have with another person, the brain starts to think what that other person must be thinking. Have you ever caught yourself assuming what someone will think, react, or say? If you've agreed with what I've said until now, how can you be so sure that what you assume someone else is thinking is right?

The brain is the deal-breaker part of our body that differentiates us from other species. It is, however, a very fickle organ. It makes us believe the most peculiar things. It convinces us that we saw stuff that wasn't really there. It can even rewrite our memory. For example, a study has been conducted in which people were shown holiday pictures in Disneyland where Bugs Bunny shakes hands with the kids. After the slideshow was over, some subjects clearly remembered shaking Bugs Bunny's hand as well when they were in Disneyland, even though Bugs Bunny never appeared in Disneyland. He is a Warner Brothers character.

My goal here is to illustrate that it is not advisable to try to guess what someone else thinks. It is not advisable to blindly believe even your own thoughts. I don't want to pull the rug out from under your feet, but the quicker you accept that your mind should be questioned from time to time, the better decision-maker you'll become. The better decisions you make, the fewer regrets you'll have. The fewer regrets you have, the less mental clutter, negativity, pain, sorrow, anger, and frustration you'll have to deal with. And bang, here you've reached the state you've been looking for, the goal you had in mind when you bought this book—a rewired mind.

"This is all good, and you made my heart race with this pep-talk, Steven, but I still don't know how to get there, how to know what to ignore, how to make better decisions, and have less headaches, mental clutter, and a rewired mind," you might think.

Or not. I might be wrong about what you think. But if I'm right, then don't worry—in the following chapters, I will talk about your brain's function, how to keep your most annoying mental habits under control, and how to let go of those mental hiccups you can't control.

Chapter 1: Two Minds and Two Brains

Zen Buddhism differentiates two types of mind: the thinking mind and the observing mind. The first type is the voice is your head that relentlessly blabs, and even if you decide to meditate and quiet your thoughts, it still will project some thoughts. The thinking mind never sleeps. It chatters to you when you queue, when you're about to sleep, and sometimes even while you're sleeping. Have you ever noticed this? Yes? Then you did it with your observing mind.

The observing mind is the one you should use to keep track of your thoughts and actions. Unfortunately, people don't use their observing minds very often. It is an unnatural activity to be conscious about the observing mind all the time. Until I read about Zen Buddhism, I didn't even know it existed. I didn't call it my "observing mind." Mostly I referred to it as my better judgment, or my "right mind." Usually, I wasn't in my right mind. When someone cries out to you saying, "What were you thinking? You're not in your right mind!" that person actually means, "Hey, you! Please check upon your thinking mind with your observing mind, because it's running wild!"

When the thinking mind gets out of control, the observing mind can't do much about it. Have you ever asked someone for help with how to channel your anger? "What can I do to stop feeling angry?"

The answer is you can't stop it. Once the thinking mind gets unchained, that horse is gone. What you can do is to not relate with your emotions. Zen teaches that instead of telling yourself "I am angry," you should say, "I feel anger." You are not the human form of anger; you've just been poisoned by this emotion. By reframing your thoughts, you'll distance yourself from the emotion.[iii]

The Biological Structure of Your Two Minds

As I mentioned in the previous chapter, the evolutionary timeline of the human brain started with the brain stem. It is positioned atop the spinal cord. This primitive brain is responsible for the metabolism of the organs, and for controlling motion and different reactions. The emotional centers emerged from this primitive brain hundreds of thousands of years later. Even later still, the neocortex—the thinking brain—evolved from these emotional centers.[iv]

Without meaning to confuse you, I will now introduce two types of brains. While in Zen we differentiate the thinking and observing minds, here we will talk about the emotional brain and the thinking brain.

Based on neuropsychological data, one thing is clear: our emotional brain is millions of years ahead of our thinking brain. On the yearly calendar of human brain evolution, the neocortex appeared sometime in December. Therefore, emotional reactions as basic instincts are much more present in our subconscious than rational reactions.

The first layer of the ancient emotional cells atop the brainstem was responsible for analyzing smells. In other words, the first kind of emotion ever felt was generated by smelling. The olfactory lobe—or as I call it, the smelling brain—helped us survive by allowing us to distinguish nutritious smells from poisonous ones, as well as the difference between the smells of a friend, sexual partner, or foe, and helped us to identify all the scents carried by the wind.

The second layer of the emotional brain was responsible for sending messages to the entire nervous system about what the body should do: get closer, run away, bite, throw, chase, etc.

As the first mammals appeared, new brain layers evolved, which formed a small half-circle around the brain stem. We call this brain the limbic system. The limbic system is responsible for more complex emotions such as love, hate, anger, or sorrow. The limbic system, as opposed to the previous brain structure, has two important features: *it can learn and store memories*. Thanks to these features, our reactions became more refined and adaptable. For example, if a shelter proved to be overly exposing and dangerous, next time, we knew to avoid it.

The last change in the brain's evolutionary timeline happened about one hundred million years ago, when on top of the thin two-layered cortex (the emotional brain), other layers of brain cells developed. These new layers formed the neocortex, which compared to the old cortex, had a distinguishing, extraordinary thinking ability. The human neocortex interprets what the old cortex's senses perceive. It allows us to have thoughts about our thoughts and feelings.

The cortex and the neocortex are connected and intertwined via countless circuits. Thus the emotional center has a strong influence over the thinking brain.[v]

Emotions vs. Reactions

What is the main difference between a long-distance and a short-distance runner? They have the same task—they have to run. However, they have different goals. The short-distance runner has to run as fast as they can to succeed. The long-distance runner, on the other hand, has to think about how to preserve their energy, so they run much more slowly than a short-distance runner, but at a constant and sustainable speed.

The same happens with your emotional brain and thinking brain. The emotional brain is much quicker to react. If your thoughts are a 100-meter dash, the emotional brain will run it much faster than the thinking brain. By the time the thinking brain reaches the target, the emotional brain is already having a nap there—if you're lucky. If you're unlucky, it ran an extra hundred meters, becoming even more troublesome for the thinking brain to catch up to.

Evolutionarily speaking, the swift emotional brain was essential for survival. In a split-second, the emotional brain had to decide if danger was around. If the rational brain would have started to analyze the situation, taking into consideration all the sensible factors to make a decision, you might have ended up dead.

A byproduct of the speed of the emotional mind is a strong sense of conviction that follows the emotional reaction. It is not enough to make an emotionally based fight-or-flight reaction; you have to be certain that's the good decision to make. Without a subconscious certainty, your mind wouldn't put all the nerves in your system on alert. Emotional decision-making and certainty happen before the thinking mind can even grasp what's going on. This is why you sometimes do something or say something, and only seconds later, you think, "Did I really say this out loud? What was I thinking?" That's the thing—you weren't. It was all the fault of your emotional mind, which "sacrifices accuracy for speed."[vi]

Social development happened much quicker than the evolutionary development could follow. This means that we still give those emotional responses to today's problems that we did thousands of years ago. Clearly, the fear of getting eaten by a T-Rex today is not a real one, unless you go to Jurassic World. Whatever fear you experience, in most cases, it doesn't threaten your core survival.

Paul Ekman, an American psychologist and the master of emotions and their relation to mimics, stated that the core, full-powered emotion doesn't even last longer than a few seconds. Everything that follows the appearance of an emotion is a mood connected to that particular emotion. The emotion becomes mood, and it gets sustained if its trigger is sustained. Goleman gives the example of mourning a lost loved one: the feeling of loss, missing the other person, and the thought you will never see them again perpetuates the emotion of sorrow.

If you feel angry about something, the full heat of anger lasts for a brief amount of time. Longtime anger gets sustained if you keep on recalling the reason for your anger. Sometimes you even re-evoke the bad emotion if you forget about it for some time, because you think you're entitled to express it. Let's say you got angry at your husband for walking in the kitchen with dirty shoes. During the day, you forgot about your anger and performed your everyday tasks, but when evening came and your husband got home, you recalled your morning anger by vivifying the muddy footprints burnt into your memory, and you began arguing.

Ekman says that the true nature of emotions is to last for only a brief amount of time. React to danger with fear and flight response quickly, or allow yourself to be distracted by happiness only for a little while, otherwise you can't react to ever-changing circumstances. If our ancestors got caught up in an emotion for too long, they might have failed to react to a new impulse or threat and would have been in trouble.

In many cases, the emotional brain "enslaves" the thinking brain to its benefit. The emotional brain itself cannot sustain an emotion for long, but when aided by the thinking brain, even the slightest hint of anger can be transformed into a long-running daytime soap opera. The thinking brain has the power to keep emotions "alive" for a long time. Our thoughts trigger and fuel some emotions. If we constantly think negative things like "I'm a failure" or "I'm hysterical," similar emotions will be triggered to back this up, like fear, anxiety, and anger.

How to handle this maze?

While we can't control what emotions we feel, in most cases, we can choose what kind of thoughts to have. If we learn to control our thoughts better, that will have an indirect impact on our emotional reactions. We can't prevent an emotion from showing up, but we can prevent how long it lasts. If you want to get rid of anger, you can't vow to yourself that from now on you won't feel angry anymore. This is not how emotions work. The next time you feel angry, you'll also be disappointed that you couldn't stick to your resolution. Remember the story in the previous chapter?

You have to accept that anger, for example, is not something you can eradicate from your life. Choose your battles more wisely. Don't fight against something you can't change. What you can change are the thoughts which sustain anger. Pay careful attention to the thoughts that keep you in an angry mood, and intentionally replace them with another thought.

This won't be easy. Do you know the game "Don't Think About the Pink Elephant"? The point of this game is to keep yourself from thinking about a pink elephant that has a yellow dress and dances the chicken dance. While you read the previous lines, you imagined the elephant in a red dress, dancing the chicken dance. And now you went back to check if the dress was red or yellow the first time I mentioned it. You're right, it was yellow. I wrote red intentionally to make you question your memory, which was quite easy. I bet whatever you were thinking before, now you're slightly pissed or amused about this experiment, and you are still thinking about the pink elephant in the yellow or red dress.

So intentionally not thinking about something you shouldn't think about is almost impossible, right? But here is an easy exercise, a switch of focus that if you use it, you'll be able to control your thoughts better. Change the self-talk in your head from "I don't want to think about the thoughts that make me angry" to "I want to think about the thoughts that make me happy—or hungry, or horny, or reflective"—anything but angry. This exercise might seem like another useless self-help placebo, but in fact, it is a mild form of psychological conditioning. The brain can think about one thing at a time, and you're taking advantage of it.

When you say you don't want to think about anger, you're still thinking about anger regardless of what words you use before it. The main point of the command is anger. As a result, you'll focus on anger.

If you say, "I want to think about happiness," your mental focus will be on happiness. Even if you say, "I don't want to think about happiness," you'll still be thinking of happiness. The only word that matters in your rational command is the thing you want to focus on—the opposite of the emotion you want to avoid.

This is a great exercise you can apply to controlling your emotions. But even so, there is no guarantee what emotion will you trigger. The rational mind cannot decide what to feel, but it can control your reactions. This is what differentiates humans from the other species. Even if you feel you could kill your partner for squawking again about the kitchen refurbishment, you probably won't actually go and kill them. This is an exaggerated example, but you get the gist. If you can control your reactions in this regard, be sure that you can control them in regard to a much less annoying issue as well.

Key takeaway: Don't fight the emotions. That's useless. It's like a police officer reasoning with a crazy person on the street. Strengthen the thoughts you give as a reaction to the emotions.

Emotions Are Associative

The emotional brain is associative. As I said before, the limbic system is responsible for storing memories, and it is capable of learning. For example, the first time you burn yourself, that pain associated with fire burns into your emotional memory as well, not just your skin. The next time you see a fire, even if you don't touch it, you'll feel a certain amount of discomfort. You surely won't go to touch it. Why? Because your emotional memory associated fire with pain, thus keeping you safe from danger. In this regard, your emotional memory is your superhero, always saving you.

Emotional memory stores other type of emotions as well. For example, if you get cheated on, it will be very difficult to fully trust another partner again—let alone the one who cheated on you. Whenever you see your partner texting on his or her phone, somewhere deep down, you'll start feeling an inexplicable anxiety, and you'll start fighting. You might not even be conscious that you do it because you found out about your ex's dishonesty via his or her phone 10 years ago.

Emotional memory doesn't filter its responses through objective reality, but through its own perceptions. If you perceive texting as a danger, it doesn't really matter what it is in reality. As long as you don't see with your own eyes that your partner is only talking with his or her mother, you will feel a strange anxiety.

Goleman separates two types of thinking when it comes to emotions: categorical thinking and personalized thinking.

Categorical thinking sees everything in black and white. There is no middle ground. Whenever encountering some little bump in the road, people with categorical thinking jump to the worst conclusion: "I never know how to say the right thing" or "I always mess up everything." Do you see the extreme words hidden in these convictions? "Always," "never," "everything," the "right" thing… They are the key words in a black and white vocabulary. The problem with them is that they can work as a self-fulfilling prophecy. Also, these words give a high level of emotional anxiety. It is very difficult to live up to the expectation of these extreme words, whether they are positive or negative.

For example, if you construct a belief about yourself that you always have to be the best worker of the month, that's a lot of pressure to handle. Categorical thinking in adulthood is emotionally crippling, in my opinion. Regardless of whether the extreme words are attached to a positive or negative thought, it's bad either way. Chill a bit. The world will still orbit around the sun if you miss that shot, or you fail at a presentation.

I used to be a categorical thinker. One day, when I had an argument with my wife, something clicked. She told me, "You always react the same way to..." I stopped her, saying that she was right. I always reacted like that because she gave me such a bad reputation that I started believing in it too. Then we had a long conversation about unhealthy word usage and created a black and white words vocabulary where we put all the destructive words we used, and we started to avoid them intentionally. Since then, our disagreements have become much smoother, constructive, and they are "colorful." It's not "always the same reaction."

Watch your language if you've identified yourself as a categorical thinker. Build your own black and white word dictionary to know which words to minimize in your everyday language.

The other type of emotional thinking Goleman talks about is personalized thinking. People with personalized thinking perceive that the entire universe orbits around them. They take criticism, or neutral remarks, personally. The chair kicks their legs, not vice versa. They might seem egotistical, but they are actually suffering from a lot of self-consciousness and feelings of inadequacy. That's why they seem to interpret everything as a personal attack. They have some very deep emotional memory imprinting about not being good enough. Maybe they had overachieving or negligent parents.

Personalized thinkers are the ones about whom we say, "They have a selective memory." This means they are seeking confirmation about their beliefs all the time. They try to fish out those memories which support their beliefs. For example, if they have low self-esteem, then when they get a negative remark, they will search for memories which confirm the negativity. However, the same goes for positive remarks. If they have low-self esteem and get a positive remark, they contradict it with a cartload of negative emotional memories. Think of that colleague whose work ethic you praised yesterday, who then gave you at least five reasons why he has a bad work ethic instead.

Selective emotional memory, however, isn't limited to only personalized thinkers. Everybody who is in a highly emotional state is hard to reason with, regardless of whether they are positively or negatively motivated. It doesn't matter how reasonable your argument is; it won't overwrite temporary emotional convictions. When emotionally charged, people have a great arsenal of reasons why they are right about something.

The main problem with selective emotional memory is that it's insensitive to time. When an event in someone's life takes a similar turn as it did in the past when something bad happened, that person will likely give the same emotional reaction as in the past.

For example, if your ex used criticism to emotionally blackmail, you won't easily accept criticism from your current partner either, even if he honestly tries to help you. You'll react defensively, saying, "No one will ever manipulate me again," and you'll storm off or start an argument. Half an hour later when you think things through and analyze what your partner said, you'll realize that it was far from being offensive or hurtful. You just stored criticism as something that embittered your life for a long time. This is how your emotional memory tries to save you from getting hurt again. Old habits die hard.

If emotional memories are strongly imprinted in your limbic system, you'll know what specific event triggered it. Not all emotional imprints are strong. Some are more cannily imprinted in your brain, and you're not even aware that you have that emotional imprint; therefore, you won't know when it is triggered. You'll think your reaction is justified; that it is rooted in the impulse of the moment, rather than being the manifestation of an old scar. You'll enslave your rational brain with your emotional brain to rationalize your actions in the present, remaining oblivious to the hidden actions of your emotional memory.

This is the biological and psychological reason I dared to say in the previous chapter that sometimes we really have no clue what is going on in our mind. This is why blind certainty can get us into trouble. That's why it is beneficial to question our thoughts and actions more often.

How to Question Your Thoughts in a Constructive Way

Questioning your thoughts is a form of self-criticism. Make sure that it is constructive instead of destructive.

- Be specific about what do you want to criticize yourself for.
- Avoid categorical and personalized thinking.
- Take a specific thought that needs questioning.
- Make this thought a significant one that can illustrate what your problem is and the beliefs around it that need to be changed.

For example, take something like the inability to think clearly in when you fight with your mother.

Casting the verdict that you are terrible at conflict management in general will demoralize you. It is categorical thinking. Focus on one specific emotional outburst at a time. Every emotional hijacking has a different emotional memory background.

Anger as an emotion can be triggered in many ways. If you take your check-up out of context, you might not find the reason behind what triggered the anger, and therefore, you won't be able to annihilate it. If you're angry around your mother, focus only on that, not on your road rage—they have nothing to do with one another. Acknowledge what you did well while arguing with your mother, what you did wrong, and what can you change.

To send an unmistakable message about your issue, Daniel Goleman advises to "say exactly what the problem is, what's wrong with it, or how it makes you feel and what could be changed."

Harry Levinson, a psychologist and expert on corporate and organizational behavior improvement, warned that being specific is just as important for (self-) praise as for (self-) criticism. If you don't specify a praise, you can have false assumptions and build inaccurate overconfidence. For example, if you say, "I was awesome," that's not specific, and therefore, you'll begin to think you're awesome at everything you do. Instead, say, "I did an awesome job with my presentation today." This way, you'll feel content with yourself at work, but it won't make you believe you're an awesome partner, father, or dog-trainer as well. Earn those titles with the accurate action.

When you criticize yourself, be ready to offer yourself some kind of solution to fix the problem. Make the commitment that you'll do your best to avoid that kind of behavior in the future. Without a clear path of improvement, criticism will only cause frustration. You don't need to be ready with five specific examples of solutions up your sleeve; just give yourself a direction, alternative conflict handling approaches, etc.

If you get criticism from someone else, don't take it as a personal attack. Take responsibility instead of becoming defensive. If you become too upset, resume the conversation later. Take some time to cool down and contemplate what you heard. Try to interpret criticism as an opportunity to improve.

Chapter 2: Mental Clutter

An Overloaded Mind is Less Creative

Did you ever feel like you're only a bystander in your own life? Recently I realized how often I fail to notice the simple pleasures in life. I eat food without truly tasting it. I rush by the beauties of nature, some amazing artwork, or a good-looking woman (I made an oath to be faithful, not blind) without seeing them. I have a conversation with my friends without being mentally present, and so on.

Why do I do this? I asked myself one day. *Why can't I enjoy the moment*?

Because my mind is too busy with the future. My thoughts are one step ahead of me, debating what to do next and trying to keep me on schedule. *Being on schedule is the key for reaching your optimal level of success, isn't it?* Not always. I discovered that too much pressure coming from a tight schedule can actually kill creativity and quality work.

There are good things about living in the future. For example, the morning traffic jam becomes more enjoyable if your mind wanders somewhere else. Before you know it, you've teleported to your work place. How can one find a balance? How can one think about the future without losing the moments that are worth living for? How do we keep schedules without pressure?

A study in *Psychological Science* proved that mental clutter significantly stymies creative thinking. Wandering thoughts and obsessive deadlines can diminish focus, distract from what really matters, and cause dissatisfaction. This study claims that creative or innovative thoughts prefer to invade the mind when it is clear.

To prove their point, the researchers conducted some experiments. In one, they tested the power of associative memory based on different levels of "mental loading." The subjects were divided into two groups. One group had to memorize a string of seven digits, while the other group had to memorize a string of two digits. While keeping the digits in their active memory, the subjects had to associate relevant words with a given word as fast as possible. If the given word was "spoon," they associated words like "soup," "fork," and so on. As it turned out, those people who had to remember seven digits gave slower and more generic responses than those who had to remember only two digits. The subjects who had to remember only two digits made more creative associations much quicker.

In another experiment, the researchers figured that people who had a higher mental load automatically started to look for the most common response to given questions, while those who had "less on their minds" took some time to brainstorm a more uncommon answer. The study propounded that the human mind, if cleared of spam thoughts, is more willing to search for unique solutions, but when is busy, it will automatically look for the easiest answer.

Is it better to be 100% creative all the time?

No, not really. Evolutionarily speaking, the human brain was set up to act between two extremes: explore and exploit. In other words, sometimes the brain is open, eager to learn and discover—explore. Other times, it prefers to exploit its memory and make decisions based on it. For example, if our ancestors weren't curious, we'd still live in caves, fighting with wooden sticks. If our ancestors had been overly reckless with a mindset to explore relentlessly, our species wouldn't have survived.

This prehistoric argument is true even today. Being innovative and creative all the time, always discovering, never processing or relying on your memory, can be as destructive as living on memories too much. If you try to stay in the moment all the time by emptying your mind and denying its natural need for chatter, it will backfire the same way as mental overload. It will tire you and leave you "mindless." It is good to use your memory and let your thoughts wander when you're doing something static or unworthy of attention, like sitting in a traffic jam. However, when the time comes, the creative mind should be channeled.

You might not be aware how you overload your brain with data on a daily basis. You memorize a shopping list, some useless website names that you could easily bookmark, names, dates, events… All these can reduce your mental capacity, leading to slow thinking, mental fatigue, and stress.[vii]

Four Types of Mental Clutter You Should Be Aware Of

Steve Scott in his bestselling book, *Declutter Your Mind,* identified four major causes of why your mind gets cluttered. As you saw earlier, a cluttered mind doesn't serve your best innovative interests, and even less your everyday enjoyment of life. Mental clutter keeps you from fully experiencing the special moments in life, like being present when you spend time with your kids, spouse, family, and friends. Enjoying the beauty your five senses can capture, like a good meal, nice scenery, an inviting smell, the touch of a furry friend, or the healing power of the sound of the nature is a pity to miss.

To treat a problem, you first have to identify what the real problem is. With the help of Scott's book, you'll get familiar with the symptoms of a cluttered mind.

The first and maybe most harmful reason for mental clutter is stress.

Although stress seems to be a natural byproduct of accelerated living, it should be managed and diminished as much as possible. The paradox of choice, the information overload, the expectations you put on your shoulders—these all generate stress but they are mostly avoidable. There are other stressors out there which are less easily avoidable, like workplace problems or a sickness in the family, or the status of the economy and your mortgage. These you can't really influence, but you still can't help stressing about them, right?

Stress accumulates not only in your mind, but also in your body, and can have psychosomatic effects like sleeping and eating disorders, tension in your limbs, or in some cases, depression, peptic ulcers, or stroke. "When life becomes so intense and complicated, our psyches search out escape ramps. Too much input, too much negative exposure, and too many choices can trigger a not-so-healthy coping response," Steve Scott writes in his book.

The second reason mental clutter is one of the stressors mentioned above is the paradox of choice.

The problem of the paradox of choice increased in the consumer society of the 20th and 21st centuries. We have so many options now, so much free information to digest, so many cereals to choose from, so many career options to pursue, that every time we choose something, we inevitably start thinking about what we missed out on. We constantly feel anxious and dissatisfied, brainwashed by *what ifs* and FOMOs in all areas of our lives.

We get paralyzed in a grocery store or clothing shop, debating what to buy for minutes, or even hours. Our life is stolen while agonizing over mostly unimportant choices, and the anxiety we feel after we've made the choice. No wonder high-achievers like Mark Zuckerberg or Steve Jobs fought against decision fatigue in many life areas, including clothing. They committed to wearing the same clothes every day to free up more time in their lives, instead of suffering from "I have nothing to wear" hysteria.

The third reason for mental clutter is physical clutter. This is actually a chicken and egg story: physical clutter is a manifestation of mental and emotional clutter, while physical clutter triggers mental clutter. If you cut one, the other one will get cleaner too. It is easier to start to get rid of physical clutter because it is quicker and has a greater visual impact.

The category of physical clutter is not limited to tangible physical items. Your digital clutter belongs to this group as well. The multitude of emails you get daily (promotional emails, calls to boring networking events, and so on) all radiate a sense of urgency, when in reality, they are not that important. It almost feels like every day you get twice as much new information than the day before. Hey, you still have 24 hours.

Steve Scott's fourth category is negativity bias. This kind of mindset is absolutely normal and natural. The human brain evolved by coding three mistakes, according to Rich Hanson, PhD's book, *Confronting the Negativity Bias*: "overestimating threats, underestimating opportunities and underestimating resources (for dealing with threats and fulfilling opportunities)."

As presented in the previous chapter, emotional reactions are out of our thinking brain's control and occur much more quickly than rational thoughts. Therefore, every little threat we experience can easily spill over, cluttering our thoughts with worry, anxiety, fear, and other negative expectations. Emotional reactions can't be modified with thoughts. Only the thinking brain can be retrained to think about something that doesn't fuel negative emotions more.

One Technique to Release Mental Clutter

In the beginning of my teaching career, I was a bottom-up thinker. I analyzed where I was in the moment and what I needed in order to move to the next step (for example, how to help my current class pass an exam). I didn't have any clear idea of how I wanted to achieve this. I started to read material on how to become a better teacher, but lacking an actual target, I often spent too much time browsing useless, unhelpful things. I was also anxious because I didn't know whether my knowledge and competence would be enough.

As time passed, I realized that bottom-up thinking is not helpful when it comes to personal goals. Without knowing where you are heading, you can easily get lost in the maze of mass information and uncertainty.

When I started my own business, I permanently broke up with quick and easy, but frustrating as hell, bottom-up thinking. What mindset did I adopt instead? Top-down thinking.

There are two main differences between bottom-up and top-down thinking. The former focuses on collecting information first, and based on those findings, identifies a solution or sets a goal. The latter sets a goal first, which gives a clear idea about what specific data is needed to reach the goal. The result of bottom-up thinking is unpredictable, especially in business life, and unpredictability can cause a lot of avoidable frustrations. Top-down thinking starts with the result and then is broken down into smaller actions that will secure its fulfillment. There is still a risk that the target of top-down thinking will not be reached, but chances for success are significantly higher than with bottom-up thinking.

Once you have a definite target in front of you, the way to get there becomes much easier. This doesn't mean you must stick to the target no matter what. Based on your research, your experience as the problems evolve allows you to make changes, but by approaching the problem with top-down thinking, you can be much more focused about what steps you need to take.[viii]

The top-down approach sounds complicated, but it really isn't. It's about structuring your thoughts around a given challenge, goal, or wish. Using top-down thinking will help you let go of a lot of unnecessary thoughts. If you make a good plan, you'll know exactly what to do and when to do it without getting stressed and overwhelmed by your options.

How to Create a Good Top-Down Thinking Plan

1. Know what you want to accomplish. For argument's sake, let's say that your goal is to finish a book—a non-fiction book, to be more accurate.

2. The second step is to define what will be the key takeaway of the book. For example, *how to eradicate overthinking from your life*.

3. The next step is to do a lot of research on the topic of eradicating overthinking, simplifying thoughts, decluttering the mind, and so on to get an idea of what is needed to be in the book based on the experts' opinion.

4. Add to the research all the thoughts, experiences, ideas, and solutions you have about the topic.

5. Based on the research, separate the mass amount of data into a logical order and build up 10 or 12 chapter topics.

6. Give each chapter two to four key takeaway ideas (A-B-C-D) of what the reader can benefit from.

7. Outline each idea in each chapter based on your research.

8. Start writing the book.

Now, imagine if you started to write a book with bottom-up thinking, meaning you'd start from point eight. Who knows what that book would end up being? If I don't get the result I set in point one and two, it means that I didn't do good top-down planning—or I didn't adapt to changeable circumstances. If I messed up something about the chapters in point five, and two topics have identical messages, but I didn't change them, that will make my book repetitive, slow, and dull. If I choose not to change the topic just because I planned differently, that's dumb. Top-down thinking requires flexibility to get the best results.

What did I gain from top-down thinking? First, a lot of time and peace of mind. Knowing what to do and when to do it gives the mind a break. The top-down planning of writing a book, by the way, can go on like this:

9. Write the first three chapters in the next X days.

10. Write the second three chapters in the next X days… (And so on until the book is ready. Then give yourself a few days to revise it.)

11. Send the finished work to an editor.

Points nine through 11 are the timeframe of top-down thinking. Thinking in a top-down manner when it comes to plans can make your life much easier. Your thoughts will become less cluttered and you will save time. I suggest you consider introducing top-down thinking into your life—especially when it comes to your business or career.

There are circumstances when bottom-up thinking can be more helpful—for example, when you want to create something new and complex without knowing what the outcome will actually be. From a cognitive psychology point of view, most of our senses perceive information in a bottom-up fashion. For example, the eyes take information from the environment (psychology calls this a sensory input), or in other words, we see something. That's the bottom. Then the brain processes the information, recognizes it, turns it into a familiar image, and builds up a final cognition. The same happens when we hear, taste, touch, or smell something. Our sensatory system follows a pure bottom-up structure. This means that all day, whatever we see, hear, or smell goes through bottom-up processing.

The individual elements are analyzed fi[r]
then the brain puts them together, cr[e]
larger picture. If you see flowers, smell roses, and
hear bees humming around, your brain will send
you the information that you are in a flower
garden. All these phases go on very fast; you can't
even follow the separate pieces of information
your brain collects. You'll just know that you're in
a flower garden. However, behind this realization,
there is a serious bottom-up analysis.

When we talk about less subconscious
perceptions, like planning how to earn our first
million, top-down thinking can be much more
effective.

The Clear Plate

I read a sweet story—or practice—on the website
of The Minimalists. Joshua Fields Millburn, one of
the site's founders, talks about an experiment he
is about to conduct: clearing his plate every
time.[ix] What does this mean?

A clear plate, in Millburn's context, means that he
only puts only one thing on it at a time. For

example, when he reads, he reads. He doesn't mix reading with watching TV, or reading with running on the treadmill.

He decided to have presence in every action he does. If he catches up on social media, he gives all his attention to that. If he meets friends, he is all there instead of letting his thoughts wander to his cell phone, and so on. He simply wants to reduce stress in his life and eradicate interruptions imposed by his own, or others', expectations.

"I am in control, just as you are—we must remember that. This is my life, I am in charge, and I have the freedom to do what I want," Millburn says. "I'll stay focused on the current activity, and I'll allow no interruptions. I will live my life one moment at a time."

After I read the article, I chose to try Millburn's advice. I vowed to stay inside whichever activity I did in the moment. When I read, I let a reading trance take me away. When I wrote, I totally excluded all other distractions.

In the beginning, it was quite difficult, since I'm by nature the person who likes to stack activities to save time. I'm the one who falls off the treadmill sometimes because I get too distracted flipping the page of a book, or lets his food go cold because I'm totally caught up in a Skype call. To me, forcing myself to do just one thing was extremely challenging. I thought I would be able to finish only half the things I planned for the day.

To my greatest surprise, quite the opposite happened. I read more than I would have on the treadmill, and I remembered twice as much of what I read. I could eat faster, and the food tasted better when it was warm. I gave my undivided attention to my family, and I could set a new record of calorie-burning. I also felt much more present in my life. I knew and felt the day's events. I didn't feel like I was teleported from morning to evening in a time capsule without having any memories of the day's events.

The moments in your life deserve your attention. Feeling life and feeling alive are invaluable states to be in.

Chapter 3: Overthinking

Have you ever found that you were thinking about a problem too complexly and convinced yourself in the midst of it that you couldn't do anything about it? You saw no solution. You couldn't put up with this problem because it seemed too complicated, too big of a chunk to swallow.

Even the most complicated problem has a solution. It may require some time and effort to find it, but it certainly exists. There is another reason why people often don't find solutions to their issues. People sometimes like things to be complicated. If they are complicated, we can always hide behind the excuse, "I tried, but it was just too overwhelming, too much, and too complex to deal with." Then we apply the ostrich politics and do nothing, even though the problem won't go away. It will only grow.

Why do we do this? Often the root cause of our

problem is too painful, too hard to accept, or it would require us to admit we were wrong. Other times the solution to the problem would require a step-by-step approach, breaking the solution down into smaller parts. The execution of these steps may take months or years. The time and effort needed to solve the problem may sound painful, and today's society is not comfortable with pain.

It seems easier to overthink something and conclude it has no solution than to think less and act more. "Me? I would *love* to solve this problem, but..." Fill in the rest. Is it "out of your control"? Are you "too old, young, poor, rich, busy, or tired" to do it?

Overthinking can be a good way to deter solving the problem, but it is a bitter pill to swallow. The overthinking pill comes with many undesired side-effects: anxiety, frustration, anger, powerlessness, sorrow, uncertainty, and doubt, just to name a few.

Avoiding solving a problem is another classic reason why our mind becomes cluttered. To rewire your mind, you need to ditch the habit of avoiding problem-solving.

Ostrich politics will not make the problem go away; they just create other problems on the top of the originals. Overthinking and the problems it generates make your mind cluttered and make you feel insecure and impatient. Let's see an example of overthinking.

Joe wanted to eat fries, but he didn't have any at home. It was a stormy Sunday afternoon and the market was already closed in the sleepy town he was living in. "I'll just pass by my friend Sam's place and ask for a potato. He surely has some," Joe decided. With the brilliant thought in his mind, he got dressed in boots, a jacket, and a hat, as one is supposed to dress on a stormy Sunday afternoon.

Sam lived a couple blocks away, so on his way there, Joe took the time to figure out what to say to him when he arrived. He couldn't start with asking directly for the wicked root vegetable, because *then Sam would think* he only cared for that and had no interest in visiting otherwise. He thought he should start chattering about local political issues with Sam to make him interested and ask Joe to hang around.

But it was Sunday afternoon. Sam's wife was probably home too. *She hates politics, and as a matter of fact, hates me too. She believes that I am a bad influence on Sam. And Sam, the henpecked husband he is, will surely not invite me in, but rather talk like a moron at the front door trying to give eye signals for us to continue talking later. But, then who will give me the potatoes? Why am I so angry, anyway? It's so annoying. To the heck with Sam's wife. I won't get angry because of her. No, sir,* Joe thought as he approached Sam's house, getting more and more worked up.

Joe recalled a few times when Sam turned him away because of his wife, which were some humiliating and painful memories. "Who does he think he is, anyway, rejecting me like that?" Joe grumbled on the empty street. He imagined himself asking for potatoes and Sam rejecting him again.

Joe was furious by the time he reached his friend's door. He impatiently started banging it. When Sam came to open it with a wide smile, the only thing Joe could do was yell, *"Damn your potatoes!"* Then he stormed away.

Sam wasn't entirely sure what just happened. *What potatoes? What's wrong with Joe?*

Joe's story illustrates a wicked quirk of your brain that, if you allow it, can drive you totally nuts. My father used to call it "the brain-munching bug." I just call it overthinking.

Joe was not avoiding his problem, at least. His problem was that he had no potatoes, so he found a way to get them. And while this example was a rather funny caricature of overthinking, life is filled with more serious ones.

Dan starts to feel an uncomfortable chest pain, but he ignores it to give his maximum effort at his job. He thinks it has to do with the weather changes, or other times he explains it as a symptom of dehydration or because of an extra-hectic work phase.

However, as time passes, he becomes more and more fatigued, his job performance drops, and eventually he gets replaced by a younger and quicker man. Dan now, instead of treating the problem that brought all the other miseries upon him, starts blaming the system, fate, and his bad luck while looking for a new, much worse job.

Being jobless and stressed, he ignores his chest pain to the point where he has a heart attack on the bus while rushing to a job interview. He is lucky, survives the heart attack, rethinks his life, becomes mindful, takes better care of himself, and starts his own business based on a long-cherished dream.

In this story, our hero got to a better place in the end. But was the heart attack necessary?

Thinking can be our best friend or our worst enemy.

We humans are the only mammals who can think about thoughts and feelings. This is a gift, but it can be a curse too.

Let's take a common negative feeling: anxiety. You get anxious about an exam you know you learned enough for. Still, anxiety numbs your mind and you start forgetting everything you've learned. When you can't recall something you're sure you knew this morning, you start getting even more anxious. You feel more anxiety because of your anxiety. Now that you're aware that you're anxious, and you know that anxiety makes you forget stuff, you become anxious about your anxiety. You just tripled your crippling condition. *Where's the emergency exit from this wicked building?*

Let's examine Joe's story. Joe was hungry and craving potatoes. This lacking made him impatient and tense. This tension attracted more and more tension-related memories into his mind. (Remember the section where I was talking about the pink elephant? If you don't want to think about the pink elephant, you should tell yourself something else to think about, not that you don't want to think about the pink elephant. Joe didn't read this book.) He recalled more memories that made him tense. Then the fact that he got so angry because of hated subjects like his friend's wife made him even angrier.

In his petty, self-created rage he lashed out at his friend, who had no idea what Joe was even talking about. On his way home, Joe became even angrier because of his outburst and his self-sabotaged opportunity to eat fries due to his being hangry (hungry + angry). Good job, Joe's brain, you did it! Again.

Chances are you've experienced similar overthinking spirals a few times in your life.

Find the Reason for Your Overthinking

Overthinking is born in an information-poor mental environment. Overthinking very often serves to fill in the gaps of missing information with your own assumptions. These assumptions are the children of your emotional memory, and therefore, they are subjective, biased, and past-oriented.

To stop your brain from overthinking, be brutally honest with yourself about what you know and don't know. When you see what's missing, instead of filling the gaps with your own thoughts, try to investigate the reality.

Understand your fundamental thinking habits deeply. Rock-solid understanding is the foundation for discovering where the self-

72

sabotaging functions are. Only by identifying them correctly can you change them.

Don't try to rationalize your cluttered thinking with some complex theory. The core reason for a cluttered mind is usually a very simple one. Understand these simple reasons deeply. For example, let's say you become self-conscious when you have to show up at an event that other colleagues attend. You feel a lot of pressure to fit in, be cool enough, and hit some imaginary standard of looks you have. You construct books full of problems around a simple event, and you are anxious and think for weeks about a gazillion expectations you have to meet. Sometimes you get so worked up about these issues that you lose focus of what the real problem was. In fact, you start believing that your real problem is your old suit.

The core problem isn't the suit, and neither is the event and the fear associated with it. The root problem is your lack of self-esteem. If you want to dig deeper, your self-esteem is low because you could never felt you were enough for your father. Thus, each time you have to be yourself, you stress that it won't be enough. This is the main problem, which means it won't be fixed by buying a new suit. Find a real solution to this problem.

How? Raise questions constantly to clarify and extend your understanding about your thoughts. Self-questioning leads you to the real problem. It might take several questions for you to get there.

After you find the real problem, think about targeted solutions. For example, in the case presented above, finding a therapist and working through your childhood issues could be a solution.

Getting to a core problem that causes overthinking is like an onion: there are several layers which must be peeled away. Each question answered removes a layer.

The only immutable part of life is change. Don't waste your time not changing for the better. There is room for growth and improvement all the time. Media scholars hinted that in movies, the main character is that person who has changed the most during the plot.

In order to find the core problem that causes your overthinking, first you have to get rid of all distracting, irrelevant thoughts. Peel the proverbial onion to its core. Then analyze the central issue and search for solutions to handle the mental knot.

Chapter 4: Santa and His Goblins

Even though living standards have never been better in the modern Western world, problems like anxiety, worry, anger, and dissatisfaction don't seem to cease. In fact, there has been an increase in their prevalence. These negative emotions are the byproduct of a consumerist society.

(Please read the following paragraph in your most dramatic, action-movie-trailer voice, imagining that hordes of drummers are playing a wild rhythm as you interpret each word.)

A new influence was born in the past few decades. Its power spread quicker than anything else before it, settling into every government and public institution and family home in less than half a century. It has in its power to demonetize nations, prevent or start wars, and drive people to the verge of suicide. What's more, this "new power" is perceived and used by everybody the same way, regardless of age, race, nationality, sexual orientation, and religion. It has one name. It is called *the Internet.*

Undoubtedly, the rise of the Internet was also perhaps the best thing that happened to civilization since Prometheus stole fire from the gods for us mere mortals. There are countless benefits to the Internet, from accessibility to communication, prevalence of information, extended freedom of speech (this is a debatable benefit, but let's ignore the existence of trolls for now), collaborative knowledge, enhanced entertainment, Trip Advisor, and so on.

Why should someone write about the benefits of the Internet? No one is interested in reading about the good and working things. Those don't need explanation. Now let's bring the drummers back and continue to talk about the dark side of the Internet.

The Internet is like Santa Claus: It knows if you've been good or bad, naughty or nice, where you are, and can reach you to give you presents or punishments. You'd better watch out, and you'd better not cry. As a proper Santa Claus, the

Internet has helpers too, little minions and goblins collectively called social media platforms.

Here's the problem: These social media goblins are working hard to gain the attention of Internet Santa. They do a lot of marketing work to be as present on the Internet as possible. How can a social media goblin get Internet Santa's attention? This is achieved through being observed by as many humans as possible.

Let's go a step lower on the ladder and examine the relationship between people and social media goblins. People try to get attention on social media just as much as social media wants to get attention on the Internet. Except for a very few "social-media celebrities," most people have nothing to gain by being "present" on social media. Social media, on the other hand, has a lot to gain from becoming more and more present in your life, like collecting your browsing data for advertising purposes. The more things you end up buying through social media ads, the more the site benefits from you as a user.

Did you see Mark Zuckerberg's testimony in the Senate? He was asked how the platform survives if no one pays for using Facebook. "Senator, we run ads," he replied.

We could interpret this as a good thing. Facebook helps us find products that *it knows* we're already looking for. But we can also see it as another distraction that clutters our minds. Even when we are ship-shaping our personal virtual profile, we can't stay away from the temptation to buy something.

In my opinion, one major obstacle in rewiring your brain involves social media-powered Internet ads. But there is also another aspect of social media that distracts you from reality and makes your brain into a mess. It is a form of advertisement as well, but a more subtle one: the advertisement of the "perfect people." The look good, they do fun stuff, and they are "special."

Everyday users find beautiful pictures attractive, obviously, so they wish to become similarly attractive. They feel encouraged to virtually share the highlights of their day. But by showing off their "my-life-is-better-than-yours" activities, a new generation of people has been bred to think that anything different than the highlight reel of one's life sucks.

They believe that sorrow, worry, anger, or mediocrity is not normal. This is the biggest social problem infecting millennials and the Generation Y. Look, that girl just got married in Jimmy Choo shoes and a Vera Wang dress, with a giant Tiffany ring blinding the cameras. And that other dude, he just bought the newest Tesla model directly from Elon Musk himself. And that old fellow there? Just won the lottery after 50 years of unsuccessful attempts, and now enjoys the company of that young lady. And me? I'm browsing Facebook while cleaning my parrot cage.

I clean and think. Since that cage won't clean itself, I have nothing else to do other than think, pity myself, envy everyone else, and cunningly plot how I will revenge others' Facebook happiness with my own. What should I do to *look happy* and interesting? A Facebook feed without a weekly coolness update is the feed of a sorrowful, lonely person. This is the general perception.

Put your hands on your chest and confess something to yourself. How often did you think there's something wrong with your life when you felt like dog muck, while others posted bungee jumping pictures in the Pyrenees?

How can somebody feel normal about their ordinary life when all they can see are others' extraordinary pictures posted on social media? It is almost impossible not to feel like an oddball about having a bad day, feeling sad, angry, or anxious when everybody else seems happy online.

So what do we usually do? We know that we are oddballs, but we feel compelled to mask it in front of others. So we also start posting pictures in which we look nicer than usual, our food is healthier than usual, and so on in order to keep up with the happiness Joneses. We put a lot of mental effort into these pictures and posts, and then we tremble anxiously about how well-received our post will be. If we get the amount of likes that in our perception is sufficient enough for us to seem cool, we relax for a few hours. "It's okay. I'm cool. I'm likable." But if no one reacts to our picture, we become even more anxious than before.

The compulsive chasing of virtual happiness has

become a borderline epidemic. Keeping up with the Joneses physically and virtually leaves people feeling neurotic, anxious, stressed, and inadequate.

What do you think your grandmother did when the guy who didn't become your grandfather left her? She certainly didn't pretend that everything was fine, writing a "some people don't deserve my tears; one day, they'll regret what they did to me" article in the local newspaper (a prehistoric information source) and running wild in Vegas to take pictures of herself having the time of her life. Instead, she cried, wrote her thoughts in her journal, met up with her girlfriends, discussed that stuff happens, and shortly after, she moved on without feeling too special or too weird about it.

Almost everything on social media is a distortion of reality; it is exaggerated. 99% of a person's life lies behind those pictures. The only things that get highlighted are the extremely outstanding moments.

But not only good things are shared eagerly—think about the catastrophic news you see day by day. Bad news can also trigger negative emotions in you like fear, insecurity, anxiety, and even hysteria. The commonality between positive and negative highlights lies in their power to leave an impact. Nobody would read about a simple day where nothing happened. That's not cool enough to see or read about, even though simple events compose most of our lives.

There are plenty of things out there that we can now see or know. There are myriad adventures which can shake up the average life. We want to be special so badly and search for happiness passionately, but somehow, we end up being painfully average and unhappy. And we think this is an abnormal state.

There is something that people tend to overlook in the midst of cheesy positivity books, blogs, and kitty pictures, something Mark Manson, the author of *The Subtle Art of Not Giving a F*ck*, perfectly summarized: "the desire for more positive experience is itself a negative experience. And, paradoxically, the acceptance of one's negative experience is itself a positive experience."[x]

Does this idea sound weird or inaccurate? Let me illustrate it with a physical example.

Let's say you want to carry water in your palm. You go to the beach, pick up the water, and firmly grip it to make sure you won't lose it. What happens when you grasp the water? It starts leaking out from between your fingers. The tighter your grip is, the more water you'll lose. The same thing happens when you obsessively pursue happiness, coolness, or acceptance on social media. The more you pursue a positive feeling, the less happy you become.

Obsessing about something only reveals that you lack it. The more beautiful you want to become, the uglier you'll perceive yourself to be. The richer you want to be, the poorer you'll feel. The more you crave belonging and love, the lonelier you'll feel.

"You will never be happy if you continue to search for what happiness consists of. You will never live if you are looking for the meaning of life." —Albert Camus

This doesn't mean you shouldn't care about your

life. You should aim to become your best possible self, but don't obsess over it. Do you remember which kids got a girlfriend or a boyfriend the quickest? Those who seemed disinterested. Did you notice that there are two types of achievers at a company? There are the neurotic, want-to-be-the-best people who constantly stress about securing their "bestness," and there are those who are totally laidback and couldn't care less about the outcome, yet whose efforts yield the same (if not better than) results as the former. The only difference between them is that while the first type will probably suffer a stroke at 40, the second will dance the chicken dance at the age of 90.

Did you notice that when you care less about something, somehow things fall into place and you achieve much more than you do when you obsess about it?

Why is that? Following Mark Manson's thought thread, if pursuing something positive is negative, then pursuing something negative becomes positive.[xi]

For example, the harder you train, the better

you'll look. Accepting your insecurities and learning to live with them makes you stronger. Honesty is painful sometimes, but without it, there's no trust. Respecting a diet is not easy, but the results speak for themselves. Saying no to someone is terrifying, but it gives you time for yourself. Everything of value in life has to be earned by enduring a related difficulty.

Going back to where I began this thought thread—with social media goblins, Internet Santa, and the way they can convince people that being normal is actually abnormal, and therefore bad— gray days, messy hair, pain, anger, failure, worry, averageness, and boredom are crucial aspects of life. Without them, there is no happiness or personal development. The only abnormality is trying to tear them out of your life or trying to mask them with an illusion.

The best thing you can do is ignore what you see on social media. Be aware that when you put up with social media banalities, you're competing with a fictional world. Social media with its pictures and events doesn't have any effect on your life unless you let it. It won't change who you are as a person unless you act upon it. Step out of this virtual rat race and chase the worthwhile things you actually care about instead.

Chapter 5: Improve Your Thoughts

Anything taken to an extreme can be harmful. This is also true of thinking. Thinking too much can have negative consequences. People can think small problems into big ones. They overanalyze, build up, or deconstruct meaningless stupidities until the problem grows big and scary enough to run away from.

Overthinking is harmful, even if you do it with positive things. The more you analyze a good event, the less happiness will you feel. At some point, any spark the moment created will be extinguished by obsessive thinking, and you can self-sabotage your own happiness.

What do I mean here? Let's say something good happened to you. Maybe your boyfriend took you out to a nice dinner. You've been together for a while, so you start assuming he will propose.

At this point, like in the movie *Sliding Doors*, two things can happen: A) He does propose, or B) He does not propose.

Overthinking related to option B is not hard to imagine. You'll start thinking that maybe he doesn't love you, that he'll never propose, that you're wasting your time, that he's not the one and you should break up with him, or that he wanted to make fun of you by giving you false hopes, and so on.

If option A happens and all your dreams come true, you can still overthink it: What if he changes his mind at the last minute, what if he didn't actually want to propose, what if he just gave in to your constant pressure, what if he was cheating on you and this is how he wants to feel better about himself, what if he's not the one...?

It's just a dinner. The idea of proposing is the child of overthinking already, let alone all the crazy thoughts that followed. You can see how easy it is to overthink a positive event, which in this case was a pleasant dinner with your boyfriend.

Now you might say, "Yes, you are right. To the rubbish bin with overthinking. I get it. I have to find the root cause, I have to care less about social media, care more about the things what matter... *And that's it?* Will I be cured of overthinking if I do all this?"

I can't promise that you will never overthink anything again, even if you follow everything mentioned above. But you stand a good chance of overthinking things less frequently. Here are some more tips on how you can tame your hyperactive mind.

Look at your thoughts from an airplane view

Put things into a wider perspective. When you feel that uncontrollable mental wave coming to overwhelm your right mind, quickly show it a stop sign by asking yourself: "Will this matter in five years, five weeks, or even five days?" It probably won't.

Of course, the answer depends on the situation—not everything loses its importance. Someone close to you dying, for example, will leave a void in your heart forever. But with time, even grief can ease.

However, the rude salesperson won't matter in five days. A disagreement with a good friend won't matter in five weeks. A breakup won't matter in five years.

Of course, acknowledging the time perspective won't make the present less painful, but it will help you to be present, mourn the situation in real time, cry it out, and let it go.

Some things are out of your control

Accept that you cannot control everything. Thinking things through a thousand times can be a sign of control mania. This deep need for control serves to make sure you don't make a mistake. Stuff happens; it's part of life. You can't have everything under your control, and you can't avoid failure all the time.

And you shouldn't. Failure, and the pain that follows, is a natural part of being human. Everyone you look up to has failed during their lifetime. Everyone makes mistakes.

Mistakes and failure are a part of a life where you truly stretch the boundaries of your comfort zone. Everyone you admire and who have lived lives that inspire you have failed. They made mistakes. Nobody got crucified for it. Well, at least not in the past few centuries. Try to see the bad events as valuable feedback you can learn from.

Those things which may look negative today can turn out to be invaluable to helping you succeed in the future. You can't know for sure. Your current conception of positive and negative can easily be reversed in the future. The tattoo you love today can become dull and unwanted in 10 years. Today's painful breakup might be the best thing that ever happened to you in a year. You can never know what tomorrow holds, so don't try to obsessively control the flow of today.

Browse your emotional memory when you are tired

Negative overthinking, in my experience, strikes most viciously when I'm tired. As soon as I have five minutes of rest, some unwanted, evil thoughts crawl into my mind. When I am tired, I have the clearest visions about my wife leaving

93

me, my loved ones dying, losing all my money, becoming deathly ill, and other fun stuff. Of course, somewhere deep down, my thinking brain knows that these are pure nonsense scenarios that are so harmful and silly I shouldn't even think about them. But what can I do? Fatigue just brings out my worst fears.

If you and I are similar in this regard, let me share with you how I get rid of these thoughts: I take advantage of my emotional memory and recall the last time I had these apocalyptic visions, and remind myself that nothing happened then, so why would anything happen now? Just telling my loved ones I love them, or blending a green smoothie to secure my physical health, or changing the password on my bank account can help me ease my concerns. All these actions are, of course, just painkillers, but if they help me snap out of my fatalistic overthinking fantasies, why not use them?

Ultimately, the best solution to overcome overthinking triggered by fatigue is a very simple one: rest. Sleep. Don't try to finish writing those last 200 words or correct that last test. Sleep earlier and wake earlier tomorrow.

Know the foundation of your thoughts clearly

If you can't explain something, that means you don't know it. Regularly revise your thoughts and beliefs. If you think something is fundamentally wrong or right, spend a day assuming your conviction is true and another day assuming your conviction is false, and then act accordingly. By following this practice, you'll gain wider empirical knowledge and overthink things less often. This exercise will also help you to be more tolerant of others' opinions. You can build bridges of understanding instead of walls of judgment.

For example, if you are a democrat, pretend to be a republican and live accordingly for one day. Hang out with other republicans, blend in, and ask for their opinions and beliefs. Stay totally judgment-free. Don't forget, for that day, you're a republican too. This way, you'll see which of your preconceptions are true or false.

You can try this exercise with other convictions as well, like religion—an atheist to Hindu switch, a gay to straight switch, or a smoother one, like a cat-lover to dog-lover switch.

Become your own Socrates by asking uncomfortable questions and engaging in uncomfortable tasks.

Chapter 6: How to Stop Worrying About the Future

When I am in San Francisco, I like to go to a café in Japantown. It's a quiet, dark little café with an excellent mocha latte and unreliable Internet that prevents me from getting too distracted from the book I'm reading—or writing—but it's good enough that I can do a basic Google search. I usually spend a couple of hours there, after which I go to a nearby grocery store to buy some sushi makis for lunch. After a few occasions, I became aware that I get always the same things: one plate of tuna makis and one of salmon makis.

The thing is, I don't like tuna that much. I like salmon much more. Still, for the sake of variety, I buy both of them instead of buying only salmon makis. If I had to choose only one plate, I'd choose the salmon. If I went to eat lunch twice choosing only one plate, I'd choose salmon both times. Why do I end up buying tuna, then?

For the sake of variety? What variety? Why is variety even better? Do I buy them to appreciate the salmon makis more? Having makis which are only half salmon makes them more valuable. You may wonder, "Okay, salmon makis, got it, but where are you heading with this?"

Let me get to the point: Having this seemingly useless mental chatter on my way back to the café after lunch made me realize something.

Some of the mental chatter and clutter is necessary to make you satisfied. If you are only thinking about valuable information, none of your thoughts would be truly valuable. Some unimportant mental chatter gives true value to the good thoughts. Moreover, this is how special moments in your brain will become truly special. Human beings are creatures who understand value only by comparing. How can you know that you have good thoughts? By having some bad ones and comparing them. Just like good and bad, happiness and pain, having a sometimes clear and sometimes cluttered mind is normal.

Does the mental chatter make you feel weird sometimes? Sure, it does. But this weirdness is also part of you. Some chatter will pop in your mind even when you try to clear it. Don't get upset with yourself, and don't take the chatter personally. Just acknowledge its presence and let it go. Practicing meditation at the end of the day is the part where you retreat from the present, but find your way back.

Let me clarify it now: The type of mental chatter I'm talking about here does not equal obsessive-compulsive overthinking, an unhealthy mental overload, or the harmful thoughts I talked about in previous chapters.

This kind of inner chatter is the purest, most innocent instinctive voice of yours. This voice has a childlike curiosity and a willingness to discover and understand the world for your benefit, not to mess your life up. If you want a visualize it, this voice is the proverbial angel on your shoulder. It's the voice of your true personality, part of those little quirks and perks that make you *you*. This relentless chatter will give birth to some great ideas that take you forward, instead of holding you back.

You know how can you distinguish "helpful mental chatter" from overthinking? Helpful mental chatter is followed by action. Overthinking serves mostly to avoid taking action.

Some people know what they are supposed to do, but they don't act. Others get stuck in analysis paralysis to avoid failure and pain. However, avoiding pain and failure is not helpful. This fosters them from the chance to learn. After all, a failure today can become a great success tomorrow, if you let it.

Ditch the analysis paralysis and make decisions instead. Whatever decision you make will bring you somewhere. It can be a place of success or a place to learn. Failing to make a decision means you failed to learn and grow.

Now and then, you'll hit proverbial forks in the road. When this happens, you may think that you have two options: going left or going right. The Minimalists, Joshua Fields Millburn and Ryan Nicodemus, argue that you have not two, but four choices when it comes to an existential crossroads.

The first option is what they call "the right path." This is the path of an obviously correct decision. There are no questions related to this road. It is like Sunset Boulevard, surrounded by palm trees, illuminated, and with fireworks sparking all the way around. These are choices like, "Should I hire a witch and curse my banker for mismanaging my money, or shall I solve this issue peacefully within the boundaries of the law?" Obviously, the first option is a no-no.

The other side of the obvious choices is called "the wrong path." Choices here are blatantly incorrect. If you have a little reason, a conscience, and some sensibility, you will avoid these routes. Sometimes they may seem quite tempting, like telling your annoying boss she's "an ugly toad and a sociopath, and it's no wonder she doesn't have a husband." Taking revenge on her in such a manner is a very attractive option, but you and I both know you're much better than that.

The Minimalists call the third type of choice "the left path." In many cases, one path seems right, but so does the other. Maybe you cannot tell which path is the better one. Maybe one would be good in the short-term, the other in the long-term.

This reminds me of the translation offer I once received: X dollars' advance plus 10% royalties, or no advance but 20% royalties. Clearly, for the short-term, the first option sounded more tempting. Who cares about a reward I'll receive five years from now when I can spend the money today? If you encounter such a situation in your life, the best thing you can do is to collect all the pros and cons you see today for both options. Why today? Because who knows what tomorrow brings? You can't know what your future self will wish, or how they would weigh the pros and cons. Write down all you can think of in favor of and against both choices, compare your lists, and from there make a sensible decision.

If you decided well, good job. If you picked the wrong choice, learn from it. I picked the second option, by the way, the long-term 20%. Why? Based on my needs in that moment, I didn't need quick money, fortunately. Since I didn't know how I would stand financially in five years, that 20% gave me a sense of security and peace of mind. In my case, long-term investment was a current pro.

The fourth choice is to make no choice at all. When we look at two unknown possibilities, we often freeze and start overthinking them, succumb to analysis paralysis, and avoid taking action so as not to risk failure. Not making a decision is also a decision, but it is the worst kind. It will keep you stuck and at the mercy of the rest of the world.[xii]

You Shouldn't Worry About Your Decisions Too Much

Decisions we have to make each day are connected to one single frame of time—our future.

As a matter of fact, there is no other species on Earth that anticipates future events like humans do. Squirrels may save nuts for the winter and migratory birds might fly south, but their squirrel and bird brains don't construct their futures like ours do. They are simple and driven by basic instinct, and only through sensing a decrease in temperature or waning sunlight hours do they know it is time to do what's coded in their DNA. They put together present events ("I feel cold, and it's staying darker longer") with past events ("the last time I stayed here for too long when it was cold and staying darker longer, I almost froze") to "predict" a possible consequence for the future.

Their brain doesn't jump to these conclusions based on conscious thoughts, only purely instinctual ones. Daniel Gilbert in his bestselling book, *Stumbling on Happiness*, calls these kinds of predictions "nexting."[xiii] What is nexting? It's a made-up word by Gilbert to refer to predictions such as a squirrel's nut-scavenging habits; decisions that seek short-term gratification triggered by the here and now. They are not far-reaching predictions like stock market changes, the next popular musical or painting style, or Taylor Swift's next boyfriend. Nexting is a chain of decision-making which occurs in the present moment.

You make a nexting type of decision each second. For example, while you're reading my words, you're nexting about where this thought about nexting is going. It is nexting when you instinctively bring along your umbrella when you see clouds outside. Nexting is completing a sentence that starts with "my heart will" with "go on." If we humans could only do nexting, we wouldn't be any different than a canary in a cage. A canary doesn't have any sense about the future; it just peacefully twitters, swinging on its little swing. When it's hungry, it squawks because it *knows* that food will follow. The reflex of the bird's brain is built upon the angry owner's lack of patience.

Humans are different. An unprecedented growth doubled the brain size of our ancestors, making the 1 ¼-pound brain of Homo habilis the nearly three-pound brain of Homo sapiens. Breaking down this growth to different areas, a disproportionate growth affected a certain area of the brain that we call the frontal lobe. This part of the brain, as you might have guessed from its name, is positioned above the eyes, in the front of the skull.[xiv]

In the 1800s, psychologists and neurologists assumed that the frontal lobe was a useless part of the brain which, if injured, would not result in any changes to a person's behavior. Later, in the early 1900s, their opinion changed.

Following some experiments on monkeys, psychologists and neurologists observed that lobotomizing them (chemically or mechanically destroying some parts of their frontal lobes) resulted in them becoming much calmer afterwards. The animals that were previously outraged if their food was withheld now patiently waited for their portion.

A Portuguese physician, António Egas Moniz, tried this method on human patients in the mid 1900s to treat anxiety and depression. These patients experienced the same effects as the monkeys. They felt much calmer.[xv]

As a matter of fact, they were very calm, like not having *any* worry in the world. Over the next several decades, scientists discovered damage to the frontal lobe resulted in people losing their ability to think about the future. Patients with frontal lobe damage seemed unchanged, as long as they didn't have to make any predictions about the future or have to plan. What's common to both planning and anxiety? They are future-related. Scientists today admit that humans without a healthy frontal lobe are like canaries, trapped in the eternal present and unable to "consider the self's extended existence throughout time."[xvi]

The frontal lobe, the youngest part of our brain, facilitates long-term planning. Long-term plans are those which require our attention in the form of choosing one of the four types of decisions we can make (preferably number one or three, choosing the right thing or the left thing). I also stated that making these long-term decisions shouldn't worry us too much because we don't know our future selves.

Your future self is like an ungrateful child. It doesn't matter how much you struggle to make the best possible decisions for future you—it won't be enough. Whatever you consider the best for your future self today, in a few years, it will seem rather ill-fitting or dull. And that's good. It means you grew. You have a broader perspective than you did back then, and you are less wrong about things than you were a few years before.

This doesn't mean you shouldn't choose the best option your mind can conceive today for your future self, but don't overthink it. Take it easy, because chances are that your future self "will know better," anyway.

Do you recall some opinions you held a while ago that today seem totally nutty? Yes, now you are trashing your past self, who made the best decision you could make at that moment.

I was a late bloomer. I truly believed that my first relationship would be the last and we'd always be together, having a vegetable garden and dogs. When we broke up, I thought I'd never love again. With my second girlfriend, I thought that this love was not how love was supposed to look, as though there was a standard for love. I was full of weird thoughts and decisions that, at the time, I thought served my best interests. Today, I can only laugh about them.

When my first girlfriend broke up with me, I was devastated. I believed I'd never be okay again. Boy, was I ever wrong!

I remember how frozen, broken, and depressed I was when I decided to break up with my second girlfriend. I thought the sorrow would never end and I would never be happy. I was wrong again.

Those decisions that were so painful and difficult to my past self are the best things that ever happened to my present self.

This rule works the other way around as well. Present tragedies can turn into future successes.

Put that frontal lobe to work on the best future you can conceive of today, but don't overestimate the decision's effect on your long-term life. Don't overload your mind with worries. Don't try to foresee what your future self will want. Don't overthink your options. Use the best of whatever information you have now and make a choice based on it. Your future self may or may not like your choices today, but your present heart will be at peace. That's the only thing you can aim to control. This is how you can clear your mind of future worries.

"Do what you can, with what you have, where you are." —Theodore Roosevelt

Chapter 7: The Perfect Practice

When you want to rewire your mind, it always comes down to two simple ideas: discover and commit to the essentials, and leave out all the rest.

Choose well what you want to spend thoughts and energy on. When you find the main problems you wish to solve, but you don't know how to think about them constructively, here is what you can do: break the problem down to simpler tasks with the top-down thinking method.

Let's say your main priority is to simplify your life and clear your mind of unnecessary thoughts. This is the main goal, the "top." Now we have to break this goal down to smaller, more achievable steps.

What can you instantly simplify in your life to rewire your mind?

You can minimize the time spent on your phone and other electronic devices. Internet Santa is very influential. Don't let him control your life. You can also downsize the amount of engagements you have. Fewer projects to handle will lead to fewer worries.

Practice monotasking. When you eat, just eat. When you work out, be there mentally. When you're going through your regular daily routines, focus on them.

Ease your mind by planning the next day in advance. Choose no more than three tasks for each day. Start your day with these tasks unless they are time-bound to the evening. Make sure that the three tasks you choose are relevant ones which take you from A to B. If the tasks are too complex to accomplish in one step, break them down into smaller tasks that can be accomplished in an hour or less.

Start your day with the most important task, even if you're not in the mood for it. Once you start doing it, you'll gain momentum and will have broken through the initial resistance barrier. Mood and motivation comes from starting to do something, not the other way around. If you rely on motivation to start doing a task, you'll fail to accomplish anything every time you lack motivation, which—let's face it—is the case most days.

Leo Babauta encourages having an open approach instead of following a strict schedule. This method goes against the grain of the conventional "have a schedule and work your ass off to respect it" mentality. Babauta claims that instead of keeping a schedule, it is more important to simply know your priorities and decide at the moment what you should do. If you know your priorities and how much time and energy you have available, this shouldn't be challenging. Being in the moment and focusing on the most important task according to your own priorities is much more important than completing everything on a hastily made schedule.

In his book *Power of Less,* Babauta advises asking yourself four questions about your goals:

   - Will this have an impact that will last beyond this week or month?

- How will it change my career, my relationships, and my life?
- How will this further a long-term goal of mine?
- Is that goal really important?[xvii]

Make sure the goals you are pursuing are indeed impactful, important, and worthy of your time, brain-power, and action. Don't chase a goal just for the sake of chasing it. How do you know when a goal is worth pursuing? First, if you gave an encouraging, positive answer to the four questions above, you're probably on the right track. Second, if on your path to reach the goal you can enter in a state of flow, that's another good sign.

The state of flow is achieved when you do something important. The state of flow means you lose yourself in a task and everything around you becomes dull and unimportant. It is almost a meditative state where your mind is sharp, uncluttered and focused. Professor Mihaly Csikszentmihalyi states in his book *Flow: The Psychology of Optimal Experience* that people are happiest when they are in a state of concentration, deeply absorbed in what they are doing. In this state of flow, people bury themselves so deeply in the activity that nothing else seems to matter.[xviii]

He divided a person's mental state into eight challenge and skill levels. If somebody has a low level of skill and challenge, then that person can slip into a state of apathy. For example, if you are bad at copywriting, but you have to do it sometimes at your workplace, you'll probably hate doing it. There will be no reward or praise for it, but there won't be any negative consequence either. "What's the point?" you might ask.

If the challenge level rises, but your skill level doesn't, your apathy can turn to worry or anxiety. If you're bad at copywriting, but know it is a crucial task for you to do in your position, you'll be terrified every time you have to write copy for your company. You'll worry about your job security, whether you'll be scolded or humiliated, and so on.

Medium-level skills with low to high challenge levels can result in boredom or frustration. If you're a decent copywriter, but nobody at your company cares about it, you'll become bored, feel unappreciated, and ultimately, your motivation for copywriting (and the desire to prove and improve yourself) will decrease.

If you have strong skills in something, but the stakes are not high, you'll feel relaxed. If you know you're the best, but your copywriting skills are seldom needed, you won't feel stressed. You'll know that any time a copywriting task pops up, you'll hit the standard.

With a medium challenge level and high-level skills, you'll feel in total control. The tasks are achievable with medium effort, so there is nothing to worry about.

With high skills and a high challenge level, you can reach the state of flow. For example, if you are Samsung's copywriter and you have to write marketing text that outperforms Apple's, you have to pull your trousers up, because even if you're one of the best, you're competing against the other bests. The task requires your best knowledge. You have to put yourself there 100%. This is an area for improvement, for creativity— for passion.

If you want to enter into a state of flow, choose a task that requires your highest skills, and one that is highly challenging as well. Eliminate all distractions around you. Then take a deep breath and immerse yourself into the depths of the power of your focusing brain. Don't let anything kick you out of there—no emotions, no swindling thoughts. Use the power of your thinking brain to your maximum benefit. Focus on the task and melt into it.

The first five, 10, or 30 minutes might not be the easiest or the most "flowy". As Carl Newport said in his book *So Good They Can't Ignore You,* and Mark Manson in his book *The Subtle Art of Not Giving a F*ck,* taking action fuels passion, not vice-versa.

First you have to sit down and *commit* to doing your best according to your abilities. At a certain point, you might not even realize when flow captures you, and you'll start working passionately.

Don't rely on passion to take action. Passion lives in the realm of emotions, and emotions are unreliable. Commitment and rational decision live in the world of thoughts. They are controllable. Relying on passion is like building a castle in the sand. It is always exposed to external circumstances. Its security is out of your control. Relying on pure commitment to action is like a castle made of stone—no amount of wind, waves, or aggressive seagulls can break it.

Do you think you aren't highly skilled at anything? That you can't enter a state of flow even if you want to?

I was born with natural drawing skills. I never learned it; I just knew. Compared to professional artists, my drawing skills might not be the best, but I still can enter into a state of flow when I draw. I always become better at drawing as a consequence. I quiet my mind, set a high challenge—like a Christmas gift for my spouse—and I immerse in my highest skill. I might not have the best drawing skills in the world, but compared to my other skills, it is the most innate and entertaining.

You don't have to have a collection of gold medals to consider yourself highly skilled in something. Whatever you know or can do better than everything else, or whatever you want to know or do better than everything else, that is the skill to use. If you are not at the highly skilled level yet, put your mind to work and learn and improve. Nobody is born highly skilled. There's always a shorter or longer learning curve you can't escape. And you shouldn't; life is in these learning curves.

Believe it or not, challenging your mind and pushing it to be in a flow state will actually clear it. You may have wondered why I even brought this up. I wrote about the flow state because it can calm your mind. A good challenge gives the brain something worthy of thought and makes it more focused on the task. When in a state of flow, your mind won't wander; it will be immersed in the moment. It is almost like a meditation practice.

Chapter 8: The Master of All High Skills

Life is a long practice session. Everything worthwhile requires practice. When I say "practice," you might think I mean improving some athletic skill or taking piano lessons, but more mundane things need to be practiced to become better, like communication, patience, or love.

We sometimes make the mistake of thinking only artistic or business skills require practice, like dancing or sealing the deal with a business contact. Behind these tangible skills, there are intangible skills which also require practice to improve, like focus, perseverance, self-discipline, confidence, self-awareness, and patience.

Why? Let's say you become a more skilled writer by reading a lot of books, and you've been practicing writing diligently for a long time. If you don't build up confidence along with it, you won't realize how much better you've become (self-awareness), and you won't garner the best returns. If you don't have the confidence to think your writing is good, your improved writing skills won't make you happy or more successful. You'll dwell in a lack of confidence, suffer from impostor syndrome, and you won't have the courage to publish your work. You need to cultivate the tangible and intangible skills together.

Practicing vs. learning

Thomas Sterner in the book *Practicing Mind* distinguishes the concepts of "practicing" and "learning." "Practice," in his use of the term, implies the presence of awareness and will, while "learning" doesn't. When people "practice," they commit to the willful repetition of something with the clear purpose of achieving a goal. Practice incorporates learning. However, learning something doesn't mean that you're also practicing it—or that you'll be practically skilled. For example, a brain surgeon can't practice brain surgery without learning its theory, but knowing everything about the theory of brain surgery won't be enough to allow someone to operate on brains.[xix]

Focus on the process. Just learn and do it, do it, do it. Observe (the outcome) and make adjustments (to improve and achieve the desired result). Use your final target as a steering wheel to navigate your practice, not as an indicator of your progress. Stay in the process to master what you're aiming for.

Avoid instant gratification

Instant gratification has no real lasting value. It's better to avoid it. How many things can you recall that you worked really hard for? Try to think of five, things like earning your degree, starting a business, finding the partner of your dreams, earning a promotion, writing your first book, and so on. Now think about five achievements in your life that required little effort. Can you recall them as easily as those that required a lot of effort?

The more effort you put into your goal, the more patiently you'll endure hardship and challenges, the more disciplined you'll be as you recover from failures and move on, and the happier you'll be when you finally achieve your goal. If you look back on your hard road paved with sweat and blood, you'll realize it was not so bad. What's more, it taught you many lessons, you became a better person by persevering, and you cultivated some self-esteem and self-confidence along the way. You'll realize that the road was much more fun and valuable than the goal itself.

"At what point in a flower's life, from seed to full bloom, has it reached perfection?" asked Thomas Sterner. What's the point in your life when your idealized concept of self-perfection is achieved? If you use the picture of perfection to inspire yourself, you're on board. However, if the utopia of perfection is a source of torment for you, that's a problem. If you can't find inspiration in perfection, learn to accept and love imperfection.

Sterner says that no moment is completely perfect or completely messed up. For example, if you feel you're bored, rushed, impatient, or disappointed with your flow activity, it means you disengaged from the present moment and are not in a state of flow anymore. When the mental chatter returns, it means you need to recalibrate your thoughts. Take a break and notice where your mind is focused.

Final Words

I hope from the bottom of my heart you found some seeds in this book that you can plant in the fertile parts of your brain to help you rewire your mind. By now, you know that emotions can't be controlled, so don't lose your focus by fighting them. Direct your focus to your cognitive abilities instead to find easier solutions to your problems, to stop overcomplicating your life, and to live more peacefully in general.

Using the information and techniques you learned in this book should help you shut out the voices in your head, prevent you from thinking with others' heads, improve your acceptance and understanding in your relationships, help you become more calm, and allow you to handle (not control) your emotions.

Don't sweat too much about future decisions. Don't put too much emphasis on things that don't have value in your life. Don't take yourself so seriously. Question your thoughts and practice what matters.

Remember what Napoleon Hills said: "Whatever the mind can conceive and believe, it can achieve." If your mind can conceive and believe in a less messy mental existence, with practice, patience, and perseverance, you'll achieve it.

Good luck!

Steve

Reference

Babauta, Leo. The Power of Less. Hay House. 2009.

Bar, Moshe. The New York Times. *Think Less, Think Better.* 2016. https://www.nytimes.com/2016/06/19/opinion/sunday/think-less-think-better.html?_r=0

C. A. Banyas. *Evolution and Phylogenetic History of the Frontal Lobes.* pg. 83-106 Guilford Press. 1999.

Csikszentmihaly, Mihaly. Flow. Ebury Digital. 2013.

Gilbert, Daniel. Stumbling on Happiness. Harper Perennial. 2009.

Goleman, Daniel. Emotional Intelligence. pg. 10. Bantam. 2006.

Manson, Mark. Mark Manson. *The Feedback Loop from Hell.* 2016. https://markmanson.net/feedback-loop-from-hell

McKey, Zoe. *Discipline Your Mind*. Kalash Media. 2017.

Millburn, Fields, Joshua. The Minimalists. *Clear Your Damn Plate.* 2017. http://www.theminimalists.com/plate/

Millburn, Fields, Joshua. Nicodemus, Ryan. The Minimalists. *The Right Path, Wrong Path, Left Path, and No Path.* 2017. http://www.theminimalists.com/paths/

Sivers, Derek. My Favorite Fable. Derek Sivers. 2009. https://sivers.org/horses

Sterner, Thomas M. Practicing Mind. New World Library. 2012

Suster, Mark. Both Sides. *The Benefits of Top-Down Thinking & Why it is Critical to Entrepreneurs.* 2010. https://bothsidesofthetable.com/the-benefits-of-top-down-thinking-why-it-is-critical-to-entrepreneurs-bec7789659a7

Endnotes

[i] Goleman, Daniel. Emotional Intelligence. pg. 10. Bantam. 2006.

[ii] Sivers, Derek. My Favorite Fable. Derek Sivers. 2009. https://sivers.org/horses

[iii] McKey, Zoe. *Discipline Your Mind*. Kalash Media. 2017.

[iv] Goleman, Daniel. Emotional Intelligence. Bantam. 2006.

[v] Goleman, Daniel. Emotional Intelligence. pg. 10-12. Bantam. 2006.

[vi] Goleman, Daniel. Emotional Intelligence. pg. 292. Bantam. 2006.

[vii] Bar, Moshe. The New York Times. *Think Less, Think Better*. 2016. https://www.nytimes.com/2016/06/19/opinion/sunday/think-less-think-better.html?_r=0

[viii] Suster, Mark. Both Sides. *The Benefits of Top-Down Thinking & Why it is Critical to Entrepreneurs*. 2010. https://bothsidesofthetable.com/the-benefits-of-top-down-thinking-why-it-is-critical-to-entrepreneurs-bec7789659a7

[ix] Millburn, Fields, Joshua. The Minimalists. *Clear Your Damn Plate.* 2017.
http://www.theminimalists.com/plate/
[x] Manson, Mark. Mark Manson. *The Feedback Loop from Hell.* 2016.
https://markmanson.net/feedback-loop-from-hell
[xi] Manson, Mark. Mark Manson. *The Feedback Loop from Hell.* 2016.
https://markmanson.net/feedback-loop-from-hell
[xii] Millburn, Fields, Joshua. Nicodemus, Ryan. The Minimalists. *The Right Path, Wrong Path, Left Path, and No Path.* 2017.
http://www.theminimalists.com/paths/
[xiii] Gilbert, Daniel. Stumbling on Happiness. Harper Perennial. 2009.
[xiv] C. A. Banyas. *Evolution and Phylogenetic History of the Frontal Lobes.* pg. 83-106 Guilford Press. 1999.
[xv] Gilbert, Daniel. Stumbling on Happiness. pg. 13-14. Harper Perennial. 2009.
[xvi] Gilbert, Daniel. Stumbling on Happiness. Harper Perennial. 2009.
[xvii] Babauta, Leo. The Power of Less. Hay House. 2009.
[xviii] Csikszentmihaly, Mihaly. Flow. Ebury Digital. 2013.
[xix] Sterner, Thomas M. Practicing Mind. New World Library. 2012.

Made in the USA
Middletown, DE
17 October 2018